ASIAPAC COMIC SERIES

The Sayings of
MENCIUS

Wisdom in a Chaotic Era

Edited & illustrated by
Tsai Chih Chung

Translated by
Mary Ng En Tzu

ASIAPAC • SINGAPORE

Publisher
ASIAPAC BOOKS & EDUCATIONAL AIDS (S) PTE LTD
2 Leng Kee Road
#02-08 Thye Hong Centre
Singapore 0315
Tel: 4751777, 4751773
Fax: 4796366

First published April 1991

© ASIAPAC BOOKS, 1991
ISBN 9971-985-59-4

Cover Design by Eric Yong

Typeset by Quaser Technology Pte Ltd
Printed in Singapore by
Loi Printing Pte Ltd

Publisher's Note

"Mencius was essentially an idealist..."
"Mencius spoke the truth boldly to men of power..."
"Mencius possessed strong human sympathies..."

Asiapac Comic Series brings to you the person of Mencius, his ideals and philosophies in a simple and entertaining manner in *The Sayings of Mencius* through Tsai Chih Chung's lively illustrations.

We feel honoured to have well-known cartoonist Tsai Chih Chung's permission to the translation right to his bestselling comics, we would also like to take this opportunity to thank the translator and typesetter for putting in their best efforts in the production of this series.

Other Titles in Asiapac Comic Series

The Sayings of Zhuang Zi
The Sayings of Confucius
The Sayings Of Lao Zi
Wonderful World of Animals - Vol. 1
The Book of Zen
Origins of Zen
A New Account of World Tales
Strange Tales of Liaozhai
Records of the Historian
Roots of Wisdom
The Sayings of Han Fei Zi
The Art of War

About the Editor/Illustrator

Tsai Chih Chung was born in 1948 in Chang Hwa County of Taiwan. He began drawing cartoon strips at the age 17 and worked as Art Director for Kuang Chi Programme Service in 1971. He founded the Far East Animation Production Company and the Dragon Cartoon Production Company in 1976, where he produced two cartoon films entitled *Old Master Q* and *Shao Lin Temple*.

Tsai Chih Chung first got his four-box comics published in newspapers and magazines in 1983. His funny comic characters such as the Drunken Swordsman, Fat Dragon, One-eyed Marshal and Bold Supersleuth have been serialized in newspapers in Singapore, Malaysia, Taiwan, Hong Kong, Japan, Europe, and the United States.

He was voted one of the Ten Outstanding Young People of Taiwan in 1985 and acclaimed by the media and the academic circle in Taiwan.

The comic book *The Sayings of Zhuang Zi* was published in 1986 and marked a milestone in Tsai's career. Within two years, *Zhuang Zi* went into more than 72 reprints in Taiwan and 15 in Hong Kong and has to-date sold over one million copies.

In 1987, Tsai Chih Chung published *The Sayings Of Lao Zi*, *The Sayings of Confucius* and two books based on Zen. Since then, he has published more than 20 titles, out of which 10 are about ancient Chinese thinkers and the rest based on historical and literary classics. All these books topped the bestsellers' list at one time or another. They have been translated into other languages such as Japanese, Korean, Thai. Asiapac is the publisher for the English version of these comics.

Tsai Chih Chung can be said to be the pioneer in the art of visualizing Chinese literature and philosophy by way of comics.

Introduction

The Sayings of Mencius contains stories about the life of Mencius and also various excerpts from "Mencius", one of the "Four Books" from the Confucian Classics.

The term "Confucian Classics" generally refers to the "Five Classics" and the "Four Books". While the "Five Classics" — namely the Odes (Shijing), the Book of History (Shujing), the Book of Changes (Yijing), the Spring and Autumn Annals (Chunqiu) and the Book of Rites (Liji) form the body of learning that was edited, taught and handed down by Confucius himself, the "Four Books" — namely the Analects (Lunyu), Mencius (Mengzi), the Great Learning (Daxue) and the Doctrine of the Mean (Zhongyong)represent the works of Confucius' followers, their records of his sayings, and their development of his thoughts.

"Mencius" has come down to us in seven books, containing 35,000 characters in 260 chapters. According to the historian Sima Qian,Mencius wrote and supervised the compilation of the work with his disciples after his retirement. In it, we see his deep conviction and enthusiasm for truth, his unflinching hold on his principles, his independence and his honesty of purpose.

Mencius was essentially an idealist. He cherished noble and lofty ideals in the face of a prevailing system which favoured rivalry and the triumph of might over right. Herein lies the germ of his sometimes excessive worship of antiquity. To him, Yao and Shun realized the ideals to which he had aspired.

Mencius summed up his ideas and the fundamentals of "The Way" in these two concepts — "Ren" (benevolence, goodness, compassion and love) and "Yi" (righteousness, justice, duty and responsibility). Whether for a king or for a mere man, these were, to Mencius, the cardinal virtues in human morality. Therefore, he spoke at length of the duty and responsibility of a king toward his people, rather than the duty of a liege toward his lord, as Confucius did. A true king, Mencius said, is one who sees the people as most important, who wins the throne by winning the people's hearts through love and righteousness, not by forcing the people to submit through might. Then, he also described the superior man as one who abides in the house of benevolence and walks in the path of righteousness. Such a man may not be influence by power, riches or poverty to give up his chastity and discipline, and he would not bend his principles to please others.

Mencius not only spoke the truth as he saw it, boldly, to the men in power, he also possessed strong human sympathies. He was interested, above all, in the welfare of the common people, and was passionately concerned about alleviating the lot of the poor and destitute. He said, those who would be good kings start by helping the lonely sufferers who have none to whom they can tell their needs...

If the words of this sage do not awaken something in our modern hearts, perhaps it is because we have already lost our true heart of love and our great way toward righteousness, as Mencius said.

He also said, "the whole purpose of learning is no more than seeking to recover the lost heart." Are we doing that?

Mary Ng

About the translator and the translation

Mary Ng En Tzu (Dr) is currently a lecturer in English Language and Communication Skills with the English Language Proficiency Unit at the National University of Singapore. After she obtained her B.A. Degree in English Literature and History, and her Master's and Doctorate in English Language Education from the University of Wisconsin-Madison, USA, in 1984, she returned home to Singapore to join the National University of Singapore, where she has been teaching for the last six years.

For the translation, she would like to acknowledge the following scholars and translators for their work, and especially Dr.James Legge for his inspiration:

J.L. Cranmer-Byng (ed.), *The Book of Mencius*, translated by Lionel Giles. London, 1949.

W.A.C.H. Dobson, *Mencius*. University of Toronto Press, 1963.

James Legge, The Works of Mencius, *The Chinese Classics, Volume II*. Hong Kong University Press, 1960.

Leonard A. Lyall, *Mencius*. Longmans, Green and Co., 1932.

Arthur Waley, *Three Ways of Thought in Ancient China*. George Allen and Unwin Ltd. London, 1974.

Contents

Mencius

Mencius (Meng Zi) inherited the thought and tradition of Confucius (Kong Zi). Having completed his studies under the disciples of Zi Si (Confucius' grandson), he toured the country and sought to offer advice to various princes; however, since his persuasions were not taken seriously by them, he retired from public life with his disciple Wan Zhang to write a preface to the *Odes* and the *Book of History,* to elaborate the views of Confucius, and to compile *The Works of Mencius* in seven books.

Later generations honoured Mencius as the great sage after Confucius. Han Yu of the Tang dynasty said "Yao hands down to Shun, Shun hands down to Yu, Yu hands down to Tang, Tang hands down to Wen, Wu, and the Duke of Zhou, Wen, Wu, and the Duke of Zhou hand down to Kong Zi, and Kong Zi hands down to Meng Ke, on whose death, there is no further transmission." Therefore Han Yu not only compared Mencius favourably to Confucius, but also thought that after him the transmission of the Traditional Way was interrupted.

The life of Mencius

Mencius (Meng Zi), named Ke, was born in the fourth year of the sovereign Lie (BC 372). He was a descendant of the Meng-sun family, one of the great Houses of the State of Lu. As the family dwindled, Mencius' family moved to the State of Zou.

1

Being poor, they lived in the countryside near a cemetery by the side of a mountain...

2

What fun!

3

If we don't move now, in future you will only know how to prepare funerals for others.

4

5

At that time, there was much fighting and many wars among the various princes. The strong exploited the weak and the big bullied the small.

30

Sufferings from the wars were so bad that "people exchanged their sons for meat and broke the bones of the dead for fire".

31

These ambitious aggressors, concerned only about their own profit, initiate wars everywhere and fill the land with their dead. They are truly inviting the earth to eat the flesh of man!

32

Therefore, Mencius led his disciples to tour the states in order to persuade the various princes to realize the kingly way and to achieve the ideal of a benevolent government.

33

However, the princes at that time only desired immediate profit and would not accept or employ his ideas.

34

Like Confucius, he was not given any opportunity to put his philosophy into action.

35

Therefore, in his old age, he turned to teaching and education, writing books and establishing his doctrine.

36

He wrote a preface to the *Shi* and *Shu* (the Odes and the Book of History), he elaborated the views of Confucius, and he compiled *The Works of Mencius* into seven books, in which he recorded the current activities of his time, the various academic exchanges and discourses, and his debates with other schools.

37

The Sayings
of
Mencius

The
Chapter on
King Hui of Liang

16

19

Will not and cannot

Can you clasp Mount Tai under your arms and jump over the North Sea?

No, I can't.

Can you give me a twig from that tree?

No I can't.

Jumping over the North Sea with Mount Tai under your arms is certainly impossible, but if you say you cannot help an old man break a tree branch, then it is not because you can't but because you won't.

What your ability cannot accomplish is what you can't do; what your ability can accomplish but you do not do is what you won't do. Men often say cannot when they will not.

20

The essence of valour

How dare he stand against me?

When a man strokes his sword, stares fiercely in anger and says,

He is merely displaying common valour which is only used to stand against another individual.

The greatness of valour depends not on number, but on whether or not your stand is righteous. A single man displays great valour if he upholds righteousness. A king marshalling his hosts displays little valour if his cause is unrighteous.

21

Those who would be good kings

The old and wifeless are widowers.

1

The old and husbandless are widows.

2

The old and sonless are solitaires.

3

The young and fatherless are orphans.

4

These four kinds of people are sufferers who have none to whom they can tell their needs. King Wen, who executed a benevolent government, would first protect these four groups of people.

5

The Odes says, "The rich can live well, but the lonely sufferers are to be pitied."

6

Those who would be benevolent kings start by sympathizing with the weak and helping the destitute.

22

Killing a sovereign

The
Chapter on
Gong Sun Chou

Helping the shoots to grow

Once there was a man of Song who was worried that his young corn was not growing...

The corn is growing so slowly! I'm getting really anxious...

1

2

Let me pull them up a little, to help them grow taller.

3

I'm so tired today; I've been helping my young corn to grow a bit taller.

4

How can this be possible? I must go and take a look...

5

Wah! All the shoots have withered away...

Everything under heaven is regulated. Those who have deliberately and artificially tried to assist growth will find that they have actually only hastened destruction.

Winning men

When men are subdued by force, their hearts are not truly won over; they submit just because they do not have enough strength to fight.

I've lost to you simply because I lack physical strength. No big deal!

When men are won by virtue, they submit sincerely and are glad in their hearts.

A true king is sincere. He has gained the submission of men through love, not through force. A tyrant can only claim the submission of men by force. Thus, being a pretender to kingship, men will submit to him only unwillingly.

The great Shun delighted in what was good

1. Zi Lu was glad when others told him of his faults.

2. Xia Yu would fall and bow when others gave him good counsel.

3. Shun was greater still; he delighted in sharing with other men, speaking good words and doing good deeds.

4. He could forsake himself to submit to the collective will of the people, and he would gladly learn what was good from other people.

5. As a farmer, a potter, a fisherman, and finally, even as a king, he never ceased to set himself to model after what was the best in others.

A sage never ceases to sincerely delight in what is good. Shun was great because he could learn from what was good in others, and he could also share his good with others.

29

The
Chapter on
Duke Wen of Teng

The man who bends himself can never straighten others

Zhao Jian, a minister, once made Wang Liang act as a charioteer for his favourite minion Xi. However, after a whole day of hunting, not a single bird was shot...

1

Wang Liang must be the worst charioteer under heaven!

Is that so?

2

Xi says that he could not capture anything that day because you were a poor charioteer.

I would like another opportunity to drive the chariot for him.

3

Xi agreed reluctantly after being pressed. Sure enough, in just one morning, he managed to shoot down ten birds that time...

4

The makings of a great man

Bene-volence | Decorum | Righteousness

To live in the spacious house of benevolence, to stand in the proper position of decorum, and to walk in the great path of righteousness; this is the Way of the great man.

1

When his ambition is fulfilled, he will lead others to follow his Way; if his ambition is disappointed, he will practise his Way alone.

2

Riches will not move his heart; poverty will not bend his discipline;

3

Power will not break his will.

4

Power and might does not make a great man; the truly great man is chaste, is immovable and is upright. He will continue to exercise discipline independent of his external circumstance.

The
Chapter on
Li Lou

Modelling on the ideal

1. To form squares or circles, pattern with standards.

2. To walk as a man, model upon the sages.

3. To be a king, practise the way of a king,

4. And to be a minister, practise the way of a minister. To do this, model upon Yao and Shun.

5. Not serving Yao as Shun served Yao is not to honour the sovereign; not to govern the people as Yao governed the people is to abuse the people.

Model after the sage kings, scrutinize the tyrants. To be a king or a minister, regard Yao and Shun.

38

If what I do cannot produce the response I expect,
then I should turn inward to search my heart
and examine myself.

7

Only when my own heart is upright,
then will everyone under Heaven
spontaneously respond to me.

8

The Odes says, "If you always remember to act in
harmony with the way of Heaven, you will
bring upon yourself perfect bliss."

9

In interactions, you cannot just focus on what you expect from others; you must also look at yourself to ensure that you have done all you can to be upright.

The way of peace

To know a man, watch his eyes

If you want to investigate a man's true character, there is nothing better than to observe his eyes. The eyes will not hide a man's wicked thoughts.

1

If a man's thoughts are upright, his eyes will be bright;

2

If his thoughts are wicked, his eyes will be clouded and shifty.

3

Listen to his words, and then watch his eyes; he won't be able to hide his true character.

4

Words convey thoughts, the eyes convey the soul; words give voice to the heart, the eyes image the heart. Goodness and wickedness are often illuminated in the eyes. Therefore, to know what a man is like, watch his eyes.

Man's greatest trouble

> Man's greatest trouble is...

> That he loves to teach others!

> A person who loves to teach others is often self-confident, self-satisfied and is unwilling to improve. However, in learning, if one does not improve, one will backslide; this is the trouble.

**Shun
and
filial piety**

Three things are deemed unfilial. One, encouraging your parents in unrighteousness through flattering assent; two, not providing for them in their poverty and old age by refusing to engage in official service; three, terminating sacrifices to your ancestors by not marrying and having offsprings.

1

Of the three things that are unfilial, to have no posterity is the greatest sin.

2

That is why Shun married without informing his parents — lest he should have no posterity.

3

Therefore, the superior man considers that he was just as filial though he did not inform them.

4

Marrying without informing your parents, and not being able to marry by informing are both deemed unfilial; however, in a difficult situation where one cannot both inform and get permission to marry, not informing may be an exigent strategy. Thus, Shun was still deemed to be in the right way though he did not inform his parents.

The practice of government

When Zi Chan ruled the kingdom of Zhen, he used to ferry his people across the waters of Zhen and Wei during the winter in his own carriage.

1

Mencius said,

This was kind, but this also showed that he did not understand the practice of government. If, after harvestime, he had repaired the foot-bridges in the eleventh month.

2

And he had repaired the cart-bridges in the twelfth month, then people would not have had to wade barefooted across the waters in the winter.

3

As long as the governor would administer things properly, he can even tell people to get out of his path when he is travelling abroad. Does he need to use his own carriage to ferry everyone across the waters?

A governor who wants to please everyone with small kindnesses will find that he does not have enough days for his work.

4

Interactions

If a sovereign regards his ministers as his hands and feet, his ministers will regard him as their heart and belly;

1

If a sovereign regards his ministers as his horses and dogs, his ministers will regard him as just a passerby;

2

Ha! Ha! Ha!
Ha! Ha!
Ha!
Ha!

If a sovereign regards his ministers as sod and grass, his ministers will regard him as their enemy.

3

Interactions among men may be likened to looking at a mirror, how others regard you reflects how you regard others.

The signs of the times

1

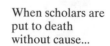
When scholars are put to death without cause...

Wah!

2
It is time for great men to leave the country.

3
When common men are slaughtered without cause...

Wah!

4
It is time for scholars to move to another place.

Before things happen, there are signs. The superior man heeds these warnings, and plans and acts before trouble closes in.

A man can do great things when he can refuse to do certain things

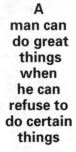

1

If a man can refuse to do certain things now...

He will be able to do great things later.

2

A successful person knows clearly the path he must follow; he will not be tempted to deviate. Thus the saying "He can do great things when he can refuse to do certain things".

Telltales

55

Never go too far

57

The superior man studies to retrieve the essentials

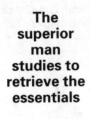

The superior man studies extensively and researches in detail...

1

In order to integrate and retrieve the essentials.

2

One pursues knowledge to gain understanding. Hence, after studying extensively, one must go on to integrate what is learnt, so that truth may be apprehended.

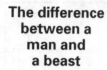

The difference between a man and a beast

1

The difference between a man and a beast is that in man there exists love and righteousness.

2

"Love and Righteousness"

While the multitudes cast away love and righteousness, the superior man protects it, knowing that it is precious.

3

The great Shun was wise. He understood the meaning of a great number of things, and he closely examined the ways of man.

4

Thus, he decided to walk in love and righteousness; not forcibly feigning it nor making use of it.

There is goodness in man; and the superior man walks in love and righteousness because it is natural to him; not because he feels he can benefit from it.

The influence of men of wisdom

1

The influence of a good sovereign ends in the fifth generation.

The influence of a mere man also ends in the fifth generation.

2

3

Although Confucius could not be my teacher,

4

Yet his virtuous influence continues. Through his disciples, I can still learn from him and so cultivate my own virtue.

The virtuous influence of ordinary men lasts but five generations; however, the influence of sages lasts ten thousand generations. For example, through me, the tradition of Confucius is passed on.

Yi had made an error

During the time of the Xia dynasty, there was a man named Feng Meng who went to learn from Yi, the lord of You Qiong, the art of shooting...

1

Soon, he had mastered all of Yi's skill in archery.

2

If I kill him, I'll be the best shot under heaven.

3

Ah!

Die now!

4

Gong Ming Yi had said, "Yi was not to be blamed." But I say, Yi had erred in this event.

5

The person of great worth

If a beautiful woman like the Lady Xi Shi was tainted and unclean...

1

Then even the people who pass by her would have to cover their noses.

How she stinks!

2

However, if a wicked man would purify and discipline himself...

3

Then even the gods will accept his sacrifices.

4

When beauty or goodness can be kept untainted it is of great value, when a man puts away his wickedness and is renewed, he is of great worth.

66

**Filial
piety**

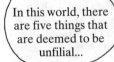 In this world, there are five things that are deemed to be unfilial...

1

The first, laziness in moving your four limbs and working to provide for your parents.

2

The second, fondness for gambling, playing chess and drinking, so that your parents are neglected.

3

The third, love of wealth and showering favours on your wife and children at the expense of your parents' needs.

4

The fourth, abandoning yourself to follow the lust of the eyes and ears so that disgrace is brought upon your parents.

5

The fifth, love of daring deeds and fights, so that your parents are burdened and are perhaps drawn into danger as well.

6

Children should look after their parents' needs at home, and they should not burden them when they are away.

Yao and Shun were ordinary men!

1. The king of Qi has sent his men to spy on you, master, to see whether you are really different from other men.

   Zhu Zi of Qi told Mencius

2. Ha! Ha! Ha! Why would I be different from other men?

3. Even Yao and Shun were ordinary men!

   There is no external difference between a sage and an ordinary man; however, they differ within; for love and righteousness reside in the heart of a sage.

Like a beggar

1. There was a man of Qi who dwelt at home with a wife and a concubine.

2. Oh! I'm so full!

Every time he goes out, he never come back unless he's been filled with wine and meat...

3. Who did you eat with?

Oh, they're all men of wealth and honour.

4. When our husband goes out, he always comes back filled with wine and meat;

And he would say that he had eaten with wealthy and honourable men. But, I've never seen a single wealthy or honourable man visit our home.

5. I think I shall follow him to see what's happening.

6. The wife got up very early the next day and begin to follow her husband secretly.

The Chapter on Wan Zhang

Deceived by what seems reasonable

1. Long ago, someone from the kingdom of Zheng gave a live fish to Zi Chan...

Keep this fish in a pond.

Yes.

2. This fish is fat and is just nice for eating, why do we still need to nurture it?

3. The officer then boiled the fish and ate it.

4. How's the fish now?

When I first put it in the pond, it didn't seem too comfortable; but after a while, it became more relaxed and swam happily to the bottom of the pond.

5. The fish has finally found its home!

Hee! Hee! Hee!

6. Who says Zi Chan is clever? I've boiled and eaten the fish already, but he still thinks that it has found its home!

It is possible to deceive a superior man by what seems reasonable, but it is impossible to deceive him by what is unreasonable.

Knowledge

When man was conceived by Heaven, the man that was first awakened to knowledge was supposed to enlighten the man who was slow in understanding;

1

And the man who was the first to apprehend The Way was supposed to instruct the man who was slow in apprehending The Way.

Those who know and sense things early, must not be selfish and make use of this advantage to pursue good only for themselves. They must go forth to instruct others.

2

The Chapter on Gao Zi

83

Using a cup of water to save a cartload of wood on fire

1 Love conquers hatred just as water subdues fire!

Hatred

2 However, those who practise love nowadays are like men who try to save a cartload of wood on fire with just a cup of water. Obviously, the fire will not be subdued.

3 So they would conclude:

Fire cannot be subdued by water!

4 By this kind of talk is the blaze of hatred encouraged so that in the end, it destroys everything; even that small amount of love.

Instead of saying that hatred cannot be subdued by love, one should try harder to love.

Rules

When Yi taught archery, he made it a rule to ensure that his bow was drawn fully;

The learner of archery too must make it a rule to do the same.

When the master-workman teaches his skill, he uses a ruler and a pair of compasses;

The learner too must follow and use the same.

There are rules in everything, whether in a little skill or in a great learning; and both the teacher and the learner must proceed according to these rules.

The
Chapter on
Jing Xin

Pursuing goodness with humility

When the great Shun dwelt among the deep mountains with the rocks and trees, and roamed with the wild pigs and the deers...

1

He was no different from the rude inhabitants of those remote mountains.

2

But when he heard a good word or a good deed, he went forth to practise it.

3

Then he was like a river that had broken forth to flow on irresistably.

4

Shun was great because he pursued goodness with humility; learning from others what is good.

Perspectives

Lu is certainly very small when viewed from the top of the mountain...

As Confucius ascended the mountains east of Lu, Lu began to look very small to him.

1

When he ascended Mount Tai, all the kingdoms below Heaven looked very insignificant.

The world seems so small when viewed from the top of Mount Tai ...

2

Therefore, those who are used to oceans find it hard to relate to others who have only seen the streams of the rivers.

3

And those who have wandered in the gates of holy men find it hard to relate to the small talk of others.

4

97

Not for three duchys would Liu Xia Hui change his course

Retaining the superior man

1
To provide food for men without loving them...

2
Is to treat men as dogs or pigs;

3
To love men without respecting them...

4
Is to treat men as domestic animals;

5
Sincere respect must exist before the offering of gifts.

6
If there is only outward respect without inward sincerity, the superior man will surely not be retained by such an empty demonstration.

Compromising "The Way" ?

When The Way is kept under Heaven, live your life according to The Way.

The Way

1

When there is no Way under Heaven, be prepared to die holding on to The Way.

The Way

2

I have never heard it said that The Way may be compromised to please others.

The Way is honourable and strict; you may follow it but you should never compromise it to please others.

3

A sage is contented in any situation

1. When Shun was but a common man, he was content to feed on plain rice and wild vegetables.

2. He lived like he did not mind if he was to be poor all his life.

3. When he became the Son of Heaven, and wore embroidered robes, played the lute and was served by Yao's two daughters, he also behaved as though he had lived in this way all his life.

4. It is as it should be!

The sage is equally comfortable in riches or in poverty. He is content in every circumstance; when he is poor, he does not complain; when he is rich, he is not proud.

Standing firm

Bad years will not starve a man who is rich in gain;

An age of corruption will not confound a man who is perfect in virtue.

Uprightness

The more one stores up, the more surplus one will have. The man who cultivates virtue and practises righteousness daily will stand firm in a crooked age.

1

2

108

The true disposition of a man who loves fame

A person who loves fame may give up a kingdom which commands a thousand chariots.

I'll let you have my kingdom of a thousand chariots.

1

Look! Am I not just like the sage kings Yao and Shun?

2

However, if this person is not truly a man who despises fame and wealth, then his face will reveal his meanness over a bowl of rice or soup.

A man who loves fame may be good at deceiving the world. His true disposition will be seen not so much in big things that require his effort as in the small things that he often pays no attention to.

3

109

People are the most important

In a kingdom, the people are the most important, next are the spirits of the land and corn, and of least importance is the sovereign.

1

Therefore, if one can gain the hearts of the people, one can become the Son of Heaven;

2

If one can gain the trust of the Son of Heaven, one can become a feudal lord;

3

And if one can gain the trust of the feudal lord, one can become an officer.

4

If a feudal lord abuses the spirits, another lord is put in his place.

If the sacrificial animals are perfect and sacrifices have been offered at the proper times, and yet droughts and floods still follow, then other altars or other spirits may be set up.

5

Man and benevolence

Constant use and practice

Mencius said to Gao Zi,

In the hills, there are footpaths...

1

If they are used very often, they become great highways.

2

But if they are not used, they soon become choked with wild grass.

3

For a long time now, your heart has not been used. It is now filled with wild grass.

4

One must constantly persevere in the pursuit of righteousness. For if one discontinues even for a moment, evil thoughts like wild grass will quickly enter to choke the heart.

Madam Feng again!

In the kingdom of Jin, there was a woman by the name of Madam Feng; she was famous for her skill in killing tigers.

1

Later, she decided to give up pounding tigers in order to be a good, gentle woman.

2

One day, she saw a crowd chasing a tiger in the wild country...

Grrr

3

Please help us.

Only you can handle this tiger.

Grrrr!

4

115

117

《亚太漫画系列》

乱世的哲思

孟子说

编著：蔡志忠
翻译：吴恩慈

亚太图书（新）有限公司出版